Positive Thoughts

Living Your Life to the Fullest

POSITIVE THOUGHTS

Living Your Life to the Fullest

Ariel Books

•

Andrews and McMeel
Kansas City

ISBN: 0-8362-0723-8

Library of Congress Catalog Card Number: 95-76436

Contents

Introduction • 7

*P*ART I:
Optimism Begins with You • *11*

*P*ART II:
The Positive Perspective • *213*

Introduction

OPTIMISM. What is this state of mind that everyone is always talking about? Doctors claim it helps people recover more quickly from illnesses. Executives encourage their salespeople to practice it. Many people repeatedly intone positive affirmations to help them achieve their goals. Whether learning to water ski or asking for a raise, we've all experienced the benefit of a positive attitude.

Looking on the bright side of things is a strategy that has been used for centuries. Is the glass half empty or half full? Becoming an optimist is a personal decision and one that has profound ramifications on how we see the world. If we think positively about ourselves, about others, and about the world around us, the world often meets our expectations.

Optimistic people tend to achieve their personal and professional goals. Think of someone you know who seems to be getting what he wants out of life. Chances are this person feels good about himself, thinks the world is a nice place, and has more friends than enemies.

How does one become an optimist? It takes

practice. The great thing about cultivating a positive outlook is that you can practice all day long without taking any extra time out of your schedule. So, the next time you're challenged, try telling yourself, "I can do it . . . I will do a great job." Before you know it, you'll be feeling more confident, more capable. The world will become sunnier and friendlier. And *you'll* be happier.

Part I

Optimism Begins with You

Keep your face to the sunshine and you cannot see the shadow.

HELEN KELLER

*Change your thoughts and
you change your world.*

NORMAN VINCENT PEALE

*S*torybook happiness involves every form of pleasant thumb twiddling; true happiness involves the full use of one's powers and talents.

John W. Gardner

14

*I*t was on my fifth birthday
that Papa put his hand on my shoulder
and said, "Remember, my son,
if you ever need a helping hand,
you'll find one at the end of your arm."

~ *Sam Levenson* ~

*S*eek not good from without: seek it within yourselves, or you will never find it.

*E*PICTETUS

To live exhilaratingly in and for the moment is deadly serious work, fun of the most exhausting sort.

~

BARBARA GRIZZUTI HARRISON

Every good thought you think is contributing its share to the ultimate result of your life.

GRENVILLE KLEISER

Don't be afraid your life will end; be afraid that it will never begin.

GRACE HANSEN

I have learned this at least by my experiment: that if one advances confidently in the direction of his dreams, and endeavors to live the life which he has imagined, he will meet with a success unexpected in common hours.

Henry David Thoreau

We have to learn to be our own best friends because we fall too easily into the trap of being our worst enemies.

Roderick Thorp

It is never too late to be what you might have been.

GEORGE ELIOT

*H*ere's one thing I've said many times to the people I've encouraged along and I hope you will remember it. If you *want* to make it, you can. You *can* move up the level system. You *can* become confident in yourself. You *can* graduate, if you *want* to.

Annabel Victoria Safire

*The important thing is
to learn a lesson
every time you lose.*

JOHN MCENROE

Happiness in the older years of life, like happiness in every year of life, is a matter of choice——your choice for yourself.

HAROLD AZINE

Never bend your head.
Always hold it high. Look
the world straight in the eye.

HELEN KELLER

*The hopeful man sees success
where others see failure,
sunshine where others see
shadows and storm.*

O. S. MARDEN

Write it in your heart that every day is the best day in the year.

~

RALPH WALDO EMERSON

It is a common experience that a problem difficult at night is resolved in the morning after the committee of sleep has worked on it.

JOHN STEINBECK

Be not afraid of life.
Believe that life is worth
living, and your belief will
help create the fact.

Henry James

For a man to achieve all that is demanded of him he must regard himself as greater than he is.

JOHANN WOLFGANG
VON GOETHE

*He that is of a merry heart
hath a continual feast.*

PROVERBS 15:15

*Be a friend to yourself,
and others will.*

SCOTTISH PROVERB

$\mathcal{Y}$our success and happiness lie in you.
External conditions are the accidents of life.
The great enduring realities are love and
service. Joy is the holy fire that keeps our
purpose warm and our intelligence aglow.
Resolve to keep happy, and your joy and you
shall form an invincible host against difficulty.

Helen Keller

I celebrate myself,
and sing myself.

WALT WHITMAN

*T*o be nobody but yourself—in a world which is doing its best, night and day, to make you everybody else—means to fight the hardest battle which any human being can fight, and never stop fighting.

e.e.cummings

*Nothing can bring you
peace but yourself.*

RALPH WALDO EMERSON

*I*f you have no confidence in self
you are twice defeated in the race of life.
With confidence, you have won even
before you have started.

Marcus Garvey

*U*nrest of spirit is a mark of life;
one problem after another presents itself
and in the solving of them we can find
our greatest pleasure.

Karl Menninger

We must accept finite
disappointment, but we must
never lose infinite hope.

~

MARTIN LUTHER KING, JR.

*For myself I am
an optimist——it does not
seem to be much use being
anything else.*

WINSTON CHURCHILL

*Neglect not the gift
that is in thee.*

I TIMOTHY 4:14

*H*e has called on the best that was in us.
There was no such thing as half-trying.
Whether it was running a race or catching
a football, competing in school—we were to try.
And we were to try harder than anyone else.
We might not be the best, and none of us were,
but we were to make the effort to be the best.
"After you have done the best you can,"
he used to say, "the hell with it."

Senator Robert F. Kennedy,
tribute to his father, Joseph P. Kennedy

No one can make you feel
inferior without your consent.

Eleanor Roosevelt

$\mathcal{I}$ don't believe in pessimism.
If something doesn't come up the way
you want, forge ahead. If you think it's
going to rain, it will.

~ *Clint Eastwood* ~

Waste no more time arguing what a good man should be. Be one.

MARCUS AURELIUS

*I*f you think you'll lose, you're lost,

For out in the world we find

Success begins with a fellow's will;

It's all in the state of mind.

*L*ife's battles don't always go

To the stronger or faster man;

But soon or late the man who wins

Is the man who thinks he can.

Walter D. Wintle

*E*verything that enlarges the sphere
of human powers, that shows man
he can do what he thought
he could not do, is valuable.

Samuel Johnson

*B*elieve that you have it,
and you have it.

(Credo quod habes, et habes.)

~

Desiderius Erasmus

$\mathcal{I}$ firmly believe that if you follow a path
that interests you, not to the exclusion of love,
sensitivity, and cooperation with others,
but with the strength of conviction that
you can move others by your own efforts, and
do not make success or failure the criteria
by which you live, the chances are you'll be
a person worthy of your own respect.

Neil Simon

I am an idealist. I don't know where I am going but I'm on my way.

❦

CARL SANDBURG

Hope is the pillar that holds up the world. Hope is the dream of a waking man.

PLINY THE ELDER

*H*ope is wanting something
so eagerly that—in spite of all
the evidence that you're not going
to get it—you go right on wanting it.
And the remarkable thing about it
is that this very act of hoping produces
a kind of strength of its own.

Norman Vincent Peale

If you're feeling good about you, what you're wearing outside doesn't mean a thing.

LEONTYNE PRICE

As I grow to understand life less and less, I learn to live it more and more.

~

JULES RENARD

*L*ong-term change requires looking
honestly at our lives and realizing
that it's nice to be needed, but not at
the expense of our health,
our happiness, and our sanity.

~ *Ellen Sue Stern* ~

I have an everyday religion
that works for me. Love yourself first
and everything else falls into line.
You really have to love yourself to get
anything done in this world.

~ *Lucille Ball* ~

*T*oday a new sun rises for me;
everything lives, everything is animated,
everything seems to speak to me of
my passion, everything invites me
to cherish it . . .

~ Anne de Lenclos ~

Trust thyself: every heart vibrates to that iron string.

R ALPH W ALDO E MERSON

$\mathcal{Y}$ou never really lose until
you quit trying.

Mike Ditka

I would have you a man of sense as well as sensibility. You will find goodness and truth everywhere you go. If you have to choose, choose truth. For that is closest to Earth. Keep close to Earth, my boy: in that lies strength. Simplicity of heart is just as necessary to an architect as for a farmer or a minister if the architect is going to build great buildings.

Ann Wright,
to her son Frank Lloyd Wright

*The best way to secure
future happiness is to be
as happy as is rightfully
possible today.*

CHARLES W. ELIOT

To fill the hour—that is happiness; to fill the hour, and leave no crevice for a repentance or an approval.

RALPH WALDO EMERSON

Happiness consists not in having much, but in being content with little.

MARGUERITE
COUNTESS OF BLESSINGTON

... *W*hatever your labors and aspirations, in the noisy confusion of life, keep peace in your soul. With all its sham, drudgery, and broken dreams, it is still a beautiful world. Be cheerful. Strive to be happy.

Max Ehrmann

Whate'er your lot may be,
Paddle your own canoe.

~

*E*DWARD *P. P*HILPOTS

Happy is the soul that has something to look backward to with pride, and something to look forward to with hope.

OLIVER G. WILSON

*I*ntegrate what you believe into every single
area of your life. Take your heart to work
and ask the most and best of everybody else.
Don't let your special character and values,
the secret that you know and no one else does,
the truth—don't let that get swallowed up
by the great chewing complacency.

Meryl Streep

*Love your friend and look
to yourself.*

~

SCOTTISH PROVERB

The greatest possession is self-possession.

~

ETHEL WATTS MUMFORD

*K*now then,
whatever cheerful and serene
Supports the mind, supports the body too:
Hence, the most vital movement mortals feel
Is hope, the balm and lifeblood of the soul.

John Armstrong

It is impossible to live a pleasant life

without living wisely, well, and justly,

and it is impossible to live wisely,

well, and justly without living pleasantly.

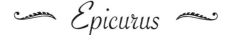 *Epicurus*

*K*eep love in your heart. A life
without it is like a sunless garden when
the flowers are dead. The consciousness
of loving and being loved brings a
warmth and richness to life that nothing
else can bring.

Oscar Wilde

I can live for two months on a good compliment.

MARK TWAIN

*Laugh at yourself first,
before anyone else can.*

~

ELSA MAXWELL

*N*ever mention the worst. Never think of it. Drop it out of your consciousness. At least ten times every day affirm, "I expect the best and with God's help will attain the best." In so doing your thoughts will turn toward the best and become conditioned to its realization.

Norman Vincent Peale

Be yourself. Who else is better qualified?

FRANK J. GIBLIN II

If you do not hope,
you will not find
what is beyond your hopes.

ST. CLEMENT OF ALEXANDRIA

$\mathcal{L}$earn what you are, and
be such.

$\mathcal{P}$INDAR

*E*very life is its own excuse for being,
and to deny or refute the untrue things
that are said of you is an error in judgment.
All wrong recoils upon the doer, and the man
who makes wrong statements about others
is himself to be pitied, not the man he vilifies.
It is better to be lied about than to lie. At the last
no one can harm us but ourselves.

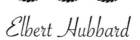

Elbert Hubbard

$\mathcal{B}$ecome a possibilitarian. No matter
how dark things seem to be or
actually are, raise your sights and see
the possibilities—always see them,
for they're always there.

~

Norman Vincent Peale

*L*ive all you can; it's a mistake
not to. It doesn't so much matter
what you do in particular so long
as you have your life.

~ *Henry James* ~

*To be able to look back
upon one's past life with
satisfaction is to live twice.*

❧

MARTIAL

Believe in life! Always human beings will live and progress to greater, broader, and fuller life.

W. E. B. Du Bois

If you think you can, you can. And if you think you can't, you're right.

MARY KAY ASH

*L*ife is a series of surprises. We do
not guess today the mood, the pleasure,
the power of tomorrow, when we are
building up our being.

~

Ralph Waldo Emerson

You don't just stumble into the future. You create your own future.

ROGER SMITH

*O*ne of the things I learned
the hard way was that it doesn't pay
to get discouraged. Keeping busy and
making optimism a way of life can
restore your faith in yourself.

~ *Lucille Ball* ~

$\mathcal{I}$f you practice an art, be proud of it and make it proud of you. . . . It may break your heart, but it will fill your heart before it breaks it: it will make you a person in your own right.

 Maxwell Anderson

When we cannot find contentment in ourselves, it is useless to seek it elsewhere.

~

*L*A *R*OCHEFOUCAULD

*The greatest mistake
you can make in life is
to be continually fearing
you will make one.*

~~~~

ELBERT HUBBARD

*A*lways give your best, never get discouraged, never be petty; always remember, others may hate you. Those who hate you don't win unless you hate them. And then you destroy yourself.

Richard M. Nixon

Great thoughts always come from the heart.

MARQUIS DE VAUVENARGUES

*H*old your head high, stick your chest out. You can make it. It gets dark sometimes but morning comes. . . . Keep hope alive.

Reverend Jesse Jackson

It takes seventeen muscles
to smile and forty-three
to frown.

~

SAYING

$\mathcal{D}$o not seek to have everything
that happens happen as you wish,
but wish for everything to happen as it
actually does happen, and your life
will be serene.

 *Epictetus*

I also know that when I'm trusting
and being myself as fully as possible,
everything in my life reflects this
by falling into place easily,
often miraculously.

~ *Shakti Gawain* ~

If it were not for hopes,
the heart would break.

THOMAS FULLER

As soon as you trust yourself, you will know how to live.

JOHANN WOLFGANG
VON GOETHE

*A*nd, above all things, never think
that you're not good enough yourself.
A man should never think that.
My belief is that in life people will take
you very much at your own reckoning.

~ *Anthony Trollope* ~

Every man is the architect
of his own fortune.

———

*E*NGLISH PROVERB

*W*hen one door shuts another opens.
He that would struggle with the world,
and bear up in adversity, ought still to resolve
not to be discouraged, for resolution is
the mother of fortitude, and not only
necessary to our support, but very much
conducive to our deliverance.

Samuel Palmer

*Everything comes to him
who hustles while he waits.*

~

THOMAS ALVA EDISON

Haggle!

*F*ear less, hope more; eat less,
chew more; whine less, breathe more;
talk less, say more; hate less, love more;
and all good things are yours.

 *Anonymous*

*I am as bad as the worst,
but, thank God, I am
as good as the best.*

WALT WHITMAN

Resolve to be thyself:
and know that he
Who finds himself,
loses his misery.

~

MATTHEW ARNOLD

*Trust your hopes,
not your fears.*

DAVID MAHONEY

K nowledge of what is
possible is the beginning
of happiness.

GEORGE SANTAYANA

$\mathcal{L}$ook, I really don't want to wax philosophic, but I will say that if you're alive, you got to flap your arms and legs, you got to jump around a lot, you got to make a lot of noise, because life is the very opposite of death. And, therefore, as I see it, if you're quiet, you're not living . . . you've got to be noisy, or at least your *thoughts* should be noisy and colorful and lively.

Mel Brooks

Laffing iz the sensation ov pheeling good all over, and showing it principally in one spot.

H. W. SHAW

Endure, and preserve your-selves for better things.

VIRGIL

He who has confidence in himself will lead the rest.

HORACE

If we spend our lives
in loving, we have no leisure
to complain, or to feel
unhappiness.

Joseph Joubert

To be a great champion
you must believe you are the
best. If you're not, pretend
you are.

~

MUHAMMAD ALI

*O*ne of the best safeguards of our hopes,
I have suggested, is to be able to mark off
the areas of hopelessness and to acknowledge
them, to face them directly, not with despair
but with the creative intent of keeping them
from polluting all the areas of possibility.

William F. Lynch

Be content with such
things as ye have.

HEBREWS 13:5

*I am as my Creator
made me, and since He is
satisfied, so am I.*

~

MINNIE SMITH

*Y*ou need to claim the events
of your life to make yourself yours.
When you truly possess all you have
been and done, which may take
some time, you are fierce with reality.

Florida Scott Maxwell

The man who makes no mistakes does not usually make anything.

EDWARD JOHN PHELPS

Happiness depends upon ourselves.

ARISTOTLE

*M*aintain a sense of perspective and proportion in all your endeavors. . . . Don't let problems and setbacks block out the light of reason. The human mind is like a magnifying glass: It exaggerates. A simple rule of thumb: Whatever you're looking at is not as big a deal as you think it is.

Daniel Meacham

Man who man would be,
must rule the empire
of himself.

PERCY BYSSHE SHELLY

*O*ne needs something to believe in,
something for which one can have
whole-hearted enthusiasm. One needs
to feel that one's life has meaning,
that one is needed in this world.

Hannah Senesh

While one person hesitates because he feels inferior, the other is busy making mistakes and becoming superior.

HENRY C. LINK

Trust thyself only, and another shall not betray thee.

THOMAS FULLER

I think these difficult times have helped me to understand better than before how infinitely rich and beautiful life is in every way and that so many things that one goes around worrying about are of no importance whatsoever.

~ *Isak Dinesen* ~

If you can't go over, you must go under.

JEWISH PROVERB

Don't try to be such a perfect girl, darling. Do the best you can without too much anxiety or strain.

JESSE BARNARD

There is nothing like a dream to create the future.

VICTOR HUGO

*Work out your
own salvation.*

PHILIPPIANS 2:12

*L*earn to get in touch with silence
within yourself and know that
everything in this life has a purpose.
There are no mistakes, no coincidences,
all events are blessings given to us
to learn from.

Elizabeth Kübler-Ross

Keep making the movements of life.

THORNTON WILDER

She didn't know it couldn't
be done so she went ahead
and did it.

MARY'S ALMANAC

It is only because of problems that we grow mentally and spiritually.

M. SCOTT PECK

*L*ive every day as if it were your last. Do every job as if you were the boss. Drive as if all other vehicles were police cars. Treat everybody else as if he were you.

~ *Phoenix Flame* ~

We know too much and feel
too little. At least we feel too little
of those creative emotions
from which a good life springs.

~ *Bertrand Russell* ~

It is not how much we have, but how much we enjoy, that makes happiness.

CHARLES HADDON SPURGEON

When you come to the end
of your rope, tie a knot
and hang on.

ATTRIBUTED TO
Franklin D. Roosevelt

When the going gets tough, the tough get going.

SAYING

Joy is what happens to us
when we allow ourselves
to recognize how good
things really are.

MARIANNE WILLIAMSON

The supreme happiness of life is the conviction that we are loved.

VICTOR HUGO

If you really do put a small
value upon yourself, rest
assured that the world will
not raise your price.

ANONYMOUS

W ithin us we have a hope
which always walks in front of
our present narrow experience; it is
the undying faith in the infinite in us.

Rabindranath Tagore

*B*e glad today.
Tomorrow may bring tears.
Be brave today. The darkest night will pass.
And golden rays will usher in the dawn.
Who conquers now shall rule the coming years.

Sarah Knowles Bolton

If I can make it,
you can make it.

REVEREND JESSE JACKSON

$\mathcal{T}$he turning point in the process
of growing up is when you discover
the core of strength within you
that survives all hurt.

~ *Max Lerner* ~

*Anything you're good at
contributes to happiness.*

BERTRAND RUSSELL

*Always look out for
the sunlight the Lord sends
into your days.*

HOPE CAMPBELL

Courage is doing what you are afraid to do. There can be no courage unless you're scared.

EDDIE RICKENBACKER

Do what you can,
with what you have,
where you are.

THEODORE ROOSEVELT

He who has health
has hope. *And* he who
has hope has everything.

~~~

ARABIAN PROVERB

*I*n doing good, avoid fame. In doing bad, avoid disgrace. Pursue a middle course as your principle. Thus you will guard your body from harm, preserve your life, fulfill your duties by your parents, and live your alloted span of life.

 *Chuangtse*

*Be cheerful
while you are alive.*

$\sim$

PTAHHOTPE

It is only with the heart
that one can see rightly;
what is essential is invisible
to the eye.

SAINT-EXUPÉRY

Make a crutch
of your cross.

ENGLISH PROVERB

The good life, as I conceive it, is a happy life. I do not mean that if you are good you will be happy; I mean that if you are happy you will be good.

 *Bertrand Russell*

*H*ope ever tells us
tomorrow will be better.

*T*IBULLUS

The more I want to get something done, the less I call it work.

RICHARD BACH

$\mathcal{D}$o not take life too
seriously. You will never
get out of it alive.

＞

$\mathcal{E}$LBERT $\mathcal{H}$UBBARD

*I*t is better to be happy

for a moment

and be burned up with beauty

than to live a long time

and be bored all the while.

Don Marquis

There is only one way to happiness
and that is to cease worrying
about things which are beyond
the power of our will.

 *Epictetus*

*H*ope, child, tomorrow
and tomorrow still,
And every tomorrow hope; trust while you live.
Hope, each time the dawn doth heaven fill,
Be there to ask as God is there to give.

Victor Hugo

It is as healthy to enjoy
sentiment as to enjoy jam.

G. K. CHESTERTON

The trick is not how much pain you feel—but how much joy you feel. Any idiot can feel pain. Life is full of excuses to feel pain, excuses not to live, excuses, excuses, excuses.

Erica Jong

*The greatest wealth is
to live content with little,
for there is never want
where the mind is satisfied.*

LUCRETIUS

*Respect yourself if you would
have others respect you.*

❦

BALTASAR GRACIÁN

*F*ind expression for a sorrow,
and it will become dear to you.
Find expression for a joy, and
you will intensify its ecstasy.

~ *Oscar Wilde* ~

Whatever comes, let's be
content withall:
Among God's blessings
there is no one small.

~ *Robert Herrick* ~

*Happiness is a habit—
cultivate it.*

ELBERT HUBBARD

$\mathcal{Y}$ou don't get to choose how you're going to die. Or when. You can only decide how you're going to live. Now.

 *Joan Baez*

I like living. I have sometimes been
wildly, despairingly, acutely miserable,
racked with sorrow, but through it all I
still know quite certainly that just to
be alive is a grand thing.

 *Agatha Christie*

You win some, you lose some, and some get rained out, but you gotta suit up for them all.

J. ASKENBERG

You have to believe in
happiness or happiness
never comes.

~

DOUGLAS MALLOCH

The one important thing I have learned over the years is the difference between taking one's work seriously and taking one's self seriously. The first is imperative and the second is disastrous.

Will Durant

*A*bove all, challenge yourself.
You may well surprise yourself at
what strengths you have, what
you can accomplish.

Cecile M. Springer

*H*e who cannot rest, cannot work;

he who cannot let go, cannot hold on;

he who cannot find footing,

cannot go forward.

Harry Emerson Fosdick

Confront the dark parts of yourself,
and work to banish them with illumination
and forgiveness. Your willingness to wrestle
with your demons will cause your angels
to sing. Use the pain as fuel, as a reminder
of your strength.

August Wilson

$\mathcal{I}$t's such an act of optimism to get through a day and enjoy it and laugh and do all that without thinking about death. What spirit human beings have!

~ *Gilda Radner* ~

Don't wish me happiness—I don't expect to be happy . . . it's gotten beyond that somehow. Wish me courage and strength and a sense of humor—I will need them all.

Anne Morrow Lindbergh

*S*ome men go through life absolutely
miserable because, despite the most enormous
achievement, they just didn't do one thing—
like the architect who didn't build St. Paul's.
I didn't quite build St. Paul's, but I stood on
more mountaintops than possibly I deserved.

Lord Thorneycroft (Peter Thorneycroft)

To hope is to enjoy.

JACQUES DELILLE

The first and great commandment is, Don't let them scare you.

ELMER DAVIS

$\mathcal{L}$ ife can be wildly tragic at times, and I've had my share. But whatever happens to you, you have to keep a slightly comic attitude. In the final analysis, you have got not to forget to laugh.

Katharine Hepburn

*If at first you don't succeed,
try, try again.*

~

SAYING

Never let the fear of striking out get in your way.

George Herman
"Babe" Ruth

oday's students] can put dope in their veins or hope in their brains. . . . If they can conceive it and believe it, they can achieve it. They must know it is not their aptitude but their attitude that will determine their altitude.

Reverend Jesse Jackson

*S*elf-help must precede help from others. Even for making certain of help from heaven, one has to help oneself.

Morarji R. Desai

*F*irst ask yourself: What is
the worst that can happen? Then
prepare to accept it. Then proceed
to improve on the worst.

Dale Carnegie

*Life is worth
living . . . since it is
what we make it . . .*

WILLIAM JAMES

$\mathcal{W}$here your pleasure is,
there is your treasure; where
your treasure, there your heart; where
your heart, there your happiness.

~ *St. Augustine* ~

*L*ike an ox-cart driver in monsoon season or the skipper of a grounded ship, one must sometimes go forward by going back.

~ *John Barth* ~

*Compassion for myself is
the most powerful healer
of them all.*

THEODORE ISAAC RUBIN

May we never let the things we can't have,
or don't have, or shouldn't have, spoil
our enjoyment of the things we do have
and can have. As we value our happiness let us
not forget it, for one of the greatest lessons
in life is learning to be happy without
the things we cannot or should not have.

Richard L. Evans

The brave man is not
he who feels no fear,
For that were stupid and irrational;
But he, whose noble soul its fears subdues,
And bravely dares the danger
nature shrinks from.

Joanna Baillie

Hope to the end.

1 PETER 1:13

*I*f I were asked to give what I consider the single most useful bit of advice for all humanity, it would be this: Expect trouble as an inevitable part of life, and when it comes, hold your head high, look it squarely in the eye and say, "I will be bigger than you. You cannot defeat me."
Then repeat to yourself the most comforting of all words,
"This too shall pass."
Maintaining self-respect in the face of a devastating experience is of prime importance.

Ann Landers

$\mathcal{T}$he secret of] how to live
without resentment or embarrassment
in a world in which I was different from
everyone else . . . was to be indifferent
to that difference.

 *Al Capp*

*Joy is the echo of
God's life within us.*

JOSEPH MARMION

The inner side of every cloud
Is bright and shining;
Therefore I turn my clouds about,
And always wear them inside out,
To show the lining.

Ellen Thornycroft Fowler Felkin

I live, which is the main point.

HEINRICH HEINE

*Y*ou're gonna have your ups and downs and your moments when you call it quits. You gotta stick it out, because there's only one ball-game here, and it's your own life. You got no choice. You got to play to win if you want to stay on this earth.

advice given to cancer patient James Brown by another patient

*No man knows what
he can do till he tries.*

PUBLILIUS SYRUS

Take plenty of time to count your blessings, but never spend a minute in worry.

ANONYMOUS

$\mathcal{D}$on't be sad, don't be angry, if life deceives you! Submit to your grief—your time for joy will come, believe me.

Aleksandr Sergeyevich Pushkin

Do continue to believe that
with your feeling and your work you
are taking part in the greatest; the more
strongly you cultivate in yourself this
belief, the more will reality and the
world go forth from it.

Rainer Maria Rilke

*Be happy. It is a way
of being wise.*

~

COLETTE

When I look in the glass I see that every line in my face means pessimism, but in spite of my face—that is my experience—I remain an optimist.

 *Richard Jefferies*

*D*o not craze yourself
with thinking, but go about
your business anywhere. Life is not
intellectual and critical, but sturdy.

Ralph Waldo Emerson

... *Y*our ability to go through life
successfully will depend largely
upon your travelling with courage
and a good sense of humor, for both
are conditions of survival. ...

~ *John R. Silber* ~

There is a real magic in enthusiasm.
It spells the difference between
mediocrity and accomplishment. . . . It
gives warmth and good feeling to all
your personal relationships.

Norman Vincent Peale

*Anyone's a fool who
doesn't try to live up to
his dreams and abilities.*

SAYING

Joy makes us giddy.

G. E. LESSING

Part II

〜

The Positive Perspective

*No matter how far
you have gone on a wrong
road, turn back.*

TURKISH PROVERB

*This is the best day
the world has ever seen.
Tomorrow will be better.*

R. A. CAMPBELL

Little deeds of kindness,
little words of love,
Help to make earth happy
like the heaven above.

JULIA A. FLETCHER CARNEY

*The world is round
and the place which may
seem like the end may also
be the beginning.*

IVY BAKER PRIEST

*Earth's crammed
with heaven.*

❧

ELIZABETH BARRETT BROWNING

The year's at the spring
And day's at the morn;
Morning's at seven;
The hillside's dew-pearled;
The lark's on the wing;
The snail's on the thorn:
God's in his heaven—
All's right with the world.

Robert Browning

*Those who bring sunshine
to the lives of others cannot
keep it from themselves.*

JAMES M. BARRIE

Gray skies are just clouds
passing over.

~

DUKE ELLINGTON

*N*ever stop. One always
stops as soon as something
is about to happen.

PETER BROOK

*When faced with a
decision, I always ask,
"What would be
the most fun?"*

PEGGY WALKER

*A*nyone can carry his burden,
however hard, until nightfall. Anyone can do
his work, however hard, for one day.
Anyone can live sweetly, patiently, lovingly,
purely, till the sun goes down. And this
is all that life really means.

attributed to Robert Louis Stevenson
by Senator Sam Erwin

The most beautiful thing in the world is, of course, the world itself.

WALLACE STEVENS

One ne must act in painting
as in life, directly.

➤

PABLO PICASSO

Open your eyes! The world is still intact; it is as pristine as it was on the first day, as fresh as milk!

PAUL CLAUDEL

Life is a short affair;
We should try to make it
smooth, and free from strife.

EURIPIDES

I've never seen
a monument erected to
a pessimist.

PAUL HARVEY

*S*tand up straight.
*A*dmire the world. *R*elish the
love of a gentle woman.
*T*rust in the *L*ord.

JOHN CHEEVER

In this best of all possible worlds . . . all is for the best.

VOLTAIRE

*L*ove makes people look at
the bright side of things. They do see
the bad things, but they make a great
effort to see the good, so they
do see the good.

 *Anonymous*

'Tis always morning
somewhere.

~

HENRY WADSWORTH
LONGFELLOW

*N*o pessimist ever discovered
the secrets of the stars, or sailed
to an uncharted land, or opened
a new heaven to the human spirit.

 *Helen Keller*

When things go wrong—
don't go with them.

ANONYMOUS

But friendship is precious,
not only in the shade, but in
the sunshine of life; and thanks to a
benevolent arrangement of things,
the greater part of life is sunshine.

President Thomas Jefferson

The world is so full of
a number of things,
I'm sure we should all be
as happy as kings.

ROBERT LOUIS STEVENSON

*M*ake a rule, and pray to God to help you to keep it, never, if possible, to lie down at night without being able to say: "I have made one human being at least a little wiser, or a little happier, or at least a little better this day."

~ *Charles Kingsley* ~

*Flowers grow out
of dark moments.*

CORITA KENT

*Trust men, and they will
be true to you; treat them
greatly, and they will show
themselves great.*

RALPH WALDO EMERSON

Life is a great big canvas;
throw all the paint on it you

can.

~

Danny Kaye

*A baby is God's opinion
that life should go on.*

~

CARL SANDBURG

It is the formidable character of
the species to routinely seek the improbable,
the difficult, even the impossible, as a source
of pleasure and self-justification. Who would
try to write poems, or novels, or paint pictures
unless he is an optimist?

Lionel Tiger

Laughter makes good blood.

ITALIAN PROVERB

How good is man's life, the mere living! how fit to employ All the heart and the soul and the sense forever in joy!

~

ROBERT BROWNING

*While there's life
there's hope.*

ENGLISH PROVERB, BORROWED
FROM CICERO

Let me win, but if I cannot win, let me be brave in the attempt.

~

SPECIAL OLYMPICS MOTTO

*W*e are all here for a spell;
get all the good laughs
you can.

WILL ROGERS

*Caring about others,
running the risk of feeling,
and leaving an impact on
people bring happiness.*

❧

RABBI HAROLD KUSHNER

Always do right. This will gratify some people and astonish the rest.

MARK TWAIN

The great pleasure in life is doing what people say you cannot do.

WALTER BAGEHOT

Be civil to all; *sociable* to many; *familiar* with few; *Friend* to one; *Enemy* to none.

❧

BENJAMIN FRANKLIN

Ideals are like stars; you will not succeed in touching them with your hands, but like the seafaring man . . . you choose them as your guides, and following them you will reach your destiny.

~ *Carl Schurz* ~

Life's a pleasant institution;
Let us take it as it comes.

W. S. GILBERT

*To be happy and contented,
count your blessings,
not your cash.*

CHINESE PROVERB

Everything that is done in the world is done by hope.

~

MARTIN LUTHER

*I*t has never been, and never will be, easy work! But the road that is built in hope is more pleasant to the traveler than the road built in despair, even though they both lead to the same destination.

Marion Zimmer Bradley

$\mathcal{T}$he best portion of

a good man's life,

His little, nameless, unremembered acts

Of kindness and of love.

~ *William Wordsworth* ~

I don't say embrace trouble.
That's as bad as treating it as an enemy.
But I do say meet it as a friend,
for you'll see a lot of it and had better
be on speaking terms with it.

Oliver Wendell Holmes, Jr.

Life is short; live it up.

NIKITA KHRUSHCHEV

*I*t is better to live one day as a lion

than a hundred years as a sheep.

(*Meglio vivere un giorno da leone*

che cento anni da pecora.)

❧

motto on Italian twenty-lire
silver piece, c. 1930

Everything is miraculous.
It is miraculous that one
does not melt in one's bath.

~

PICASSO, ATTRIBUTED

Love is all we have,
the only way that each
can help the other.

EURIPIDES

*I*f we had no winter, the spring would not be so pleasant: if we did not sometimes taste of adversity, prosperity would not be so welcome.

 *Anne Bradstreet*

*The most wasted day
of all is that on which
we have not laughed.*

SÉBASTIEN CHAMFORT

Life is still beautiful.

J. C. F. SCHILLER

Although the world is full of suffering, it is full also of the overcoming of it.

HELEN KELLER

Always do what you are afraid to do.

~

ANONYMOUS

*F*ew will have the greatness to bend history
itself; but each of us can work to change
a small portion of events, and in the total of
all those acts will be written the history
of this generation.

Senator Robert F. Kennedy

Some of the most rewarding and beautiful moments of a friendship happen in the unforeseen open spaces between planned activities. It is important that you allow these spaces to exist.

Christine Leefeldt
and Ernest Callenbach

I long to accomplish a great and noble task, but it is my chief duty to accomplish small tasks as if they were great and noble.

 *Helen Keller* ~

Walk on a rainbow trail;
walk on a trail of song,
and all about you will be beauty.
There is a way out of every dark mist,
over a rainbow trail.

Navajo song

We find a delight in
the beauty and happiness of
children, that makes the
heart too big for the body.

RALPH WALDO EMERSON

Without belittling the courage with which men have died, we should not forget those acts of courage with which men . . . have *lived*. The courage of life is often a less dramatic spectacle than the courage of a final moment; but it is no less a magnificent mixture of triumph and tragedy. A man does what he must—in spite of personal consequences, in spite of obstacles and dangers and pressures—and that is the basis of all human morality . . .

Senator John F. Kennedy

After all, tomorrow
is another day.

~

MARGARET MITCHELL

When you reach for the stars, you may not quite get them, but you won't come up with a handful of mud either.

LEO BURNETT

Don't hurry, don't worry. You're only here for a short visit. So be sure to stop and smell the flowers.

WALTER HAGEN

The way I see it, if you want the rainbow, you gotta put up with the rain.

DOLLY PARTON

*Love the moment, and
the energy of that moment
will spread beyond
all boundaries.*

CORITA KENT

Hopeful as the break of day.

THOMAS BAILEY ALDRICH

Far away there in the sunshine
are my highest aspirations. I may not
reach them but I can look up and see
their beauty, believe in them, and
try to follow them.

~ Louisa May Alcott ~

The human heart refuses
to believe in a universe
without a purpose.

~

Immanuel Kant

*Light tomorrow
with today.*

—

ELIZABETH BARRETT BROWNING

To me every hour of the light and dark is a miracle, Every cubic inch of space is a miracle.

WALT WHITMAN

Make it a rule of life never to regret and never look back. Regret is an appalling waste of energy; you can't build on it; it is good only for wallowing in.

Katherine Mansfield

Life is sweet.

ENGLISH PROVERB

Never give up on anybody.

HUBERT H. HUMPHREY

For me, a hearty "belly laugh" is one of the beautiful sounds in the world.

BENNETT CERF

It matters not how long you live, but how well.

PUBLILIUS SYRUS

*D*on't evaluate your life in terms of achievements, trivial *or* monumental, along the way. . . . Instead, wake up and appreciate everything you encounter along your path. Enjoy the flowers that are there for your pleasure. Tune in to the sunrise, the little children, the laughter, the rain, and the birds. Drink it all in . . . there is no way to happiness; happiness *is* the way.

Dr. Wayne W. Dyer

I will turn their mourning

into joy, and will comfort

them, and make them rejoice

from their sorrow.

JEREMIAH 31:13

If you shut your door to all errors, truth will be shut out.

RABINDRANATH TAGORE

Optimism doesn't wait on facts. It deals with prospects. Pessimism is a waste of time.

NORMAN COUSINS

Some people are always grumbling because roses have thorns; I am thankful that thorns have roses.

ALPHONSE KARR

Nor love thy life, nor hate;
but what thou liv'st.
Live well; how long or short
permit to Heaven.

JOHN MILTON

I have found that there is a tremendous joy in giving. It is a very important part of the joy of living.

WILLIAM BLACK

All life is an experiment.
The more experiments you
make the better.

Ralph Waldo Emerson

If you are wise, laugh.

MARTIAL

Our lives are like the course of the sun. At the darkest moment there is the promise of daylight.

LONDON TIMES

Life is real! Life is earnest!
And the grave is not its goal.

HENRY WADSWORTH
LONGFELLOW

*Make yourself necessary
to somebody.*

RALPH WALDO EMERSON

*O*ften the test of courage is
not to die but to live.

Vittorio Alfieri

*I*t just ain't possible to explain some things. It's interesting to wonder on them and do some speculation, but the main thing is you have to accept it—take it for what it is, and get on with your growing.

~ *Jim Dodge* ~

*W*hat time is it?
Time to do well,

Time to live better,

Give up that grudge,

Answer that letter,

Speak the kind word to sweeten a sorrow,

Do that kind deed you would leave 'till tomorrow.

Anonymous

Something will turn up.

BENJAMIN DISRAELI

Use no hurtful deceit; think innocently and justly and, if you speak, speak accordingly.

BENJAMIN FRANKLIN

*W*e should never despair, our situation before has been unpromising and has changed for the better, so I trust, it will again. If new difficulties arise, we must only put forth new exertions and proportion our efforts to the exigency of the times.

General George Washington

The follies which a man regrets most in his life are those which he didn't commit when he had the opportunity.

HELEN ROWLAND

Pick battles big enough to matter, small enough to win.

JONATHAN KOZOL

Take short views, hope for the best, and trust in God.

SYDNEY SMITH

Derive happiness in oneself from a good day's work, from illuminating the fog that surrounds us.

HENRI MATISSE

$\mathcal{L}$ife was meant to be lived, and curiosity must be kept alive. One must never, for whatever reason, turn his back on life.

~ *Eleanor Roosevelt* ~

$\mathcal{T}$he gloom of the world is but a shadow.
Behind it, yet within our reach, is joy. There is
radiance and glory in the darkness, could we but
see; and to see, we have only to look.
Life is so generous a giver, but we, judging its gifts by
their covering, cast them away as ugly or heavy or hard.
Remove the covering, and you will find beneath it a
living splendour, woven of love, by wisdom, with power.

Fra Giovanni

*A*ssociate yourself with men of
good quality if you esteem your own
reputation; for 'tis better to be alone
than in bad company.

George Washington

*M*ay the road rise to meet you.
May the wind be ever at your back.
May the Good Lord keep you in the hollow of His hand.
May your heart be as warm as your hearthstone.
And when you come to die
may the wail of the poor
be the only sorrow
you'll leave behind.
May God bless you always.

Anonymous

Discover day-to-day excitement.

CHARLES BAUDELAIRE

$\mathcal{T}$he most $\mathcal{I}$ can do for my
friend is simply to be his
friend.

HENRY DAVID THOREAU

To look up and not down,
To look forward and not back,
To look out and not in, and
To lend a hand.

~ *Edward Everett Hale* ~

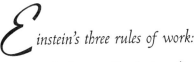

*E*instein's three rules of work:

(1) Out of clutter find simplicity.

(2) From discord make harmony.

(3) In the middle of difficulty

lies opportunity.

~ *Albert Einstein* ~

I am not a perfect servant. I am a public servant doing my best against the odds. As I develop and serve, be patient. God is not finished with me yet.

Reverend Jesse Jackson

*Don't do things to not die,
do things to enjoy living.
The by-product may be not
dying.*

~

BERNIE S. SIEGEL, M.D.

*B*e not too critical of others,
and love much.

~

JULIA HUXLEY

All of us do not have equal talent, but all of us should have an equal opportunity to develop our talent.

~

JOHN F. KENNEDY

Weeping may endure for a night, but joy cometh in the morning.

PSALMS 30:5

*L*eave tomorrow's trouble to tomorrow's strength; tomorrow's work to tomorrow's time; tomorrow's trial to tomorrow's grace and to tomorrow's God.

Anonymous

*Do not bind yourself to
what you cannot do.*

GEORGE SHELLEY

I take a simple view of living. It is keep your eyes open and get on with it.

LAURENCE OLIVIER

Keep company with those
who may make you better.

ENGLISH SAYING

$\mathcal{L}$ife is good only when it is magical and musical, a perfect timing and consent, and when we do not anatomize it. You must treat the days respectfully, you must be a day yourself, and not interrogate it like a college professor. The world is enigmatical,—everything said, and everything known or done—and must not be taken literally, but genially.

Ralph Waldo Emerson

My advice to you is not to inquire
why or whither, but just enjoy your ice
cream while it's on your plate—that's my
philosophy.

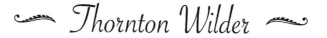 *Thornton Wilder*

Instead of loving your enemy, treat your friend a little better.

EDGAR WATSON HOWE

*Never look back unless you
are planning to go that way.*

Saying

*T*he happiest business in all the world is

that of making friends,

And no investment on the street pays larger dividends,

For life is more than stocks and bonds,

and love than rate percent,

And he who gives in friendship's name shall reap

what he has spent.

Anne S. Eaton

Wish not so much to live long as to live well.

BENJAMIN FRANKLIN

Mighty oaks from little acorns grow.

Saying

No person who is
enthusiastic about his work
has anything to fear from
life.

SAMUEL GOLDWYN

Goodness is uneventful.
It does not flash, it glows.

DAVID GRAYSON

*B*ut the nearer the dawn the darker

the night,

And by going wrong all things come right;

Things have been mended that were worse,

And the worse, the nearer they are to mend.

❧

Henry Wadsworth Longfellow

I have a simple philosophy. Fill what's empty. Empty what's full. And scratch where it itches.

ALICE ROOSEVELT LONGWORTH

The only way of finding the limits of the possible is by going beyond them into the impossible.

ARTHUR C. CLARKE

*L*ive not as though there were a thousand years ahead of you. Fate is at your elbow; make yourself good while life and power are still yours.

~ *Marcus Aurelius* ~

*N*othing is too small
to know, and nothing too big
to attempt.

WILLIAM VAN HORNE

In spite of all our hopes, dreams, and efforts, change is real and forever. Accept it fearlessly. Investigate the unknown; neither fear nor worship it.

Joseph A. Bauer

When you have only two pennies left in the world, buy a loaf of bread with one, and a lily with the other.

CHINESE PROVERB

Is life worth living? It is, so you take the risk of getting up in the morning and going through the day's work.

WALTER PERSEGATI

Happiness is like a cat. If you try to coax it or call it, it will avoid you. It will never come. But if you pay no attention to it and go about your business, you'll find it rubbing against your legs and jumping into your lap. So forget pursuing happiness. Pin your hopes on work, on family, on learning, on knowing, on loving. Forget pursuing happiness, pursue these other things, and with luck happiness will come.

William Bennett

*If you want to be loved,
love and be lovable.*

BENJAMIN FRANKLIN

*When nothing is sure,
everything is possible.*

MARGARET DRABBLE

*O*nce you have been confronted
with a life-and-death situation, trivia no
longer matters. Your perspective grows
and you live at a deeper level. There's no
time for pettiness.

*Margaretta
"Happy" Rockefeller*

*L*et us not bankrupt our todays
by paying interest on the regrets of
yesterday and by borrowing in advance
the troubles of tomorrow.

Ralph W. Sockman

*Don't fix the blame,
fix the problem.*

KEITH S. PENNINGTON

Life just is. You have to flow with it. Give yourself to the moment. Let it happen.

GOVERNOR JERRY BROWN

*The mere sense of living
is joy enough.*

EMILY DICKINSON

One of the things I keep learning is that the secret of being happy is doing things for other people.

DICK GREGORY

*Too much of a good thing
can be wonderful.*

~

Mae West

No objects of value . . . are
worth risking the priceless
experience of waking up one
more day.

❦

*J*ACK *S*MITH

*The best way out of a
difficulty is through it.*

ANONYMOUS

Life is a succession of
moments. *To* live each one
is to succeed.

CORITA KENT

Instead of allowing yourself to be so unhappy, just let your love grow as God wants it to grow; seek goodness in others, love more persons more; love them more impersonally, more unselfishly, without thought of return. The return, never fear, will take care of itself.

Henry Drummond

Do something. If it doesn't work, do something else. No idea is too crazy.

JIM HIGHTOWER

To love and be loved is to feel the sun from both sides.

DAVID VISCOTT

*L*ive full today, and let no pleasure

pass untasted—

And no transient beauty scorn;

Fill well the storehouse of the soul's delight

With light of memory—

Who knows? Tomorrow may be—Night.

 *Anonymous*

Strengthen me by sympathizing with my strength, not my weakness.

A. BRONSON ALCOTT

The only limit to our realization of tomorrow will be our doubts of today.

FRANKLIN D. ROOSEVELT

The biggest human temptation is . . . to settle for too little.

THOMAS MERTON

The tragedy of life doesn't lie in not reaching your goal. The tragedy lies in having no goal to reach.

BENJAMIN E. MAYS

*G*od loves you. God doesn't want anyone to be hungry and oppressed. He just puts his big arms around everybody and hugs them up against himself.

Norman Vincent Peale

$\mathcal{L}$et us go singing as
far as we go: the road
will be less tedious.

$\mathcal{V}$IRGIL

*W*hen it is dark enough,
you can see the stars.

*C*HARLES *A.* *B*EARD

Keep a green tree in your heart and perhaps the singing bird will come.

CHINESE PROVERB

To wish to be well is a part of becoming well.

SENECA

The thing always happens
that you really believe in;
and the belief in a thing
makes it happen.

FRANK LLOYD WRIGHT

*Problems are
only opportunities
in work clothes.*

HENRY J. KAISER

This book was typeset in Centaur MT and Savoye by Nina Gaskin.

Cover and interior design
by Judith Stagnitto Abbate